Who Was
Sacagawea?

by Judith Bloom Fradin
and Dennis Brindell Fradin

Illustrated by Val Paul Taylor

Grosset & Dunlap • New York

For our dear nieces:
Rebecca Fradin Polster, Arielle Joy Polster,
and Leslie Sharf Polster—JBF and DF

To Grandma Gwen, to my mother Charol
and to Vern—VPT

For their help, the authors thank:
Sally Freeman, Jill Harding and Curt Johnson

Library of Congress Cataloging-in-Publication Data

Fradin, Dennis B.
    Who was Sacagawea? / by Dennis Brindell Fradin and Judith Bloom Fradin ;
illustrated by Val Paul Taylor.
        p. cm.
    Summary: A brief biography of Sacagawea, the Shoshoni woman who accompanied explorers Lewis and Clark on their expedition in the early 1800s.
        1. Sacagawea—Juvenile literature. 2. Lewis and Clark Expedition (1804-1806)—Juvenile literature. 3. Shoshoni women—Biography—Juvenile literature. 4. Shoshoni Indians—Biography—Juvenile literature. [1. Sacagawea 2. Lewis and Clark Expedition (1804-1806). 3. Shoshoni Indians—Biography. 4. Indians of North America—Biography. 5. Women—Biography.] I. Taylor, Val Paul, ill. II. Title.
    F592.7.S123 F735 2002
    978.004'9745'0092—dc21

                                                    2002511789

ISBN 0-448-42485-1 (pbk)   I J

Contents

Who Was
Sacagawea?

In the year 2000, the
United States issued
a new dollar coin. Its
"heads" side shows
an American-Indian
woman. She is carry-
ing her baby.

Who is this young
mother? Her name was Sacagawea
(Sa KA ga WE a). Two hundred years ago, she
went with the Lewis and Clark expedition. The
explorers traveled across the American Northwest.
When the explorers were hungry, she found food.
When they met Indians along the way, she acted as
translator. Thanks to Sacagawea's help, the expedition was a success.

The Lewis and Clark expedition changed American history. It helped the United States settle a huge region. This area included what became the states of Idaho, Washington, and Oregon.

GREAT FALLS PORTAGE

BRITISH

COLUMBIA

OREGON COUNTRY

PACIFIC OCEAN

FORT CLATSOP (1805 – 1806)

SNAKE

SACAGAWEA'S SHOSHONE VILLAGE

MANDAN-MINNETAREE VILLAGE WHERE SACAGAWEA LIVED WITH CHARBONNEAU

MISSOURI R.

LOUISIA PURCHA 1803

N
W — E
S

Sacagawea was only 16 years old when she crossed America with her baby on her back. This is her true story.

MAP OF TRIP TO
COAST 1804-1805

ITORY

FORT MANDAN
(WINTER 1804-1805)

SAINT LOUIS

UNITED
STATES
1804

ATLANTIC
OCEAN

Chapter 1
A Shoshone Girl

Sacagawea was born in what is now Idaho, in 1789 or 1790. She was a Shoshone (Sho SHO nee) Indian. Her tribe lived along the Bitterroot Range of the Rocky Mountains. They often camped near the Snake River, so they were also called the Snake Indians.

As a child, she had many different names. This was common for young Indians. In time, she became known as Sacagawea. Sakaga means "bird," and wea means "woman," so her name means "Bird Woman." She may have been called Bird Woman because she was small and moved quickly like a bird.

Sacagawea had an older brother named Cameahwait (Ka ME ah wait). She also had another brother and a sister. Her family lived in a tent called a tipi. The Shoshone were peaceful wanderers.

SHOSHONE
VILLAGE

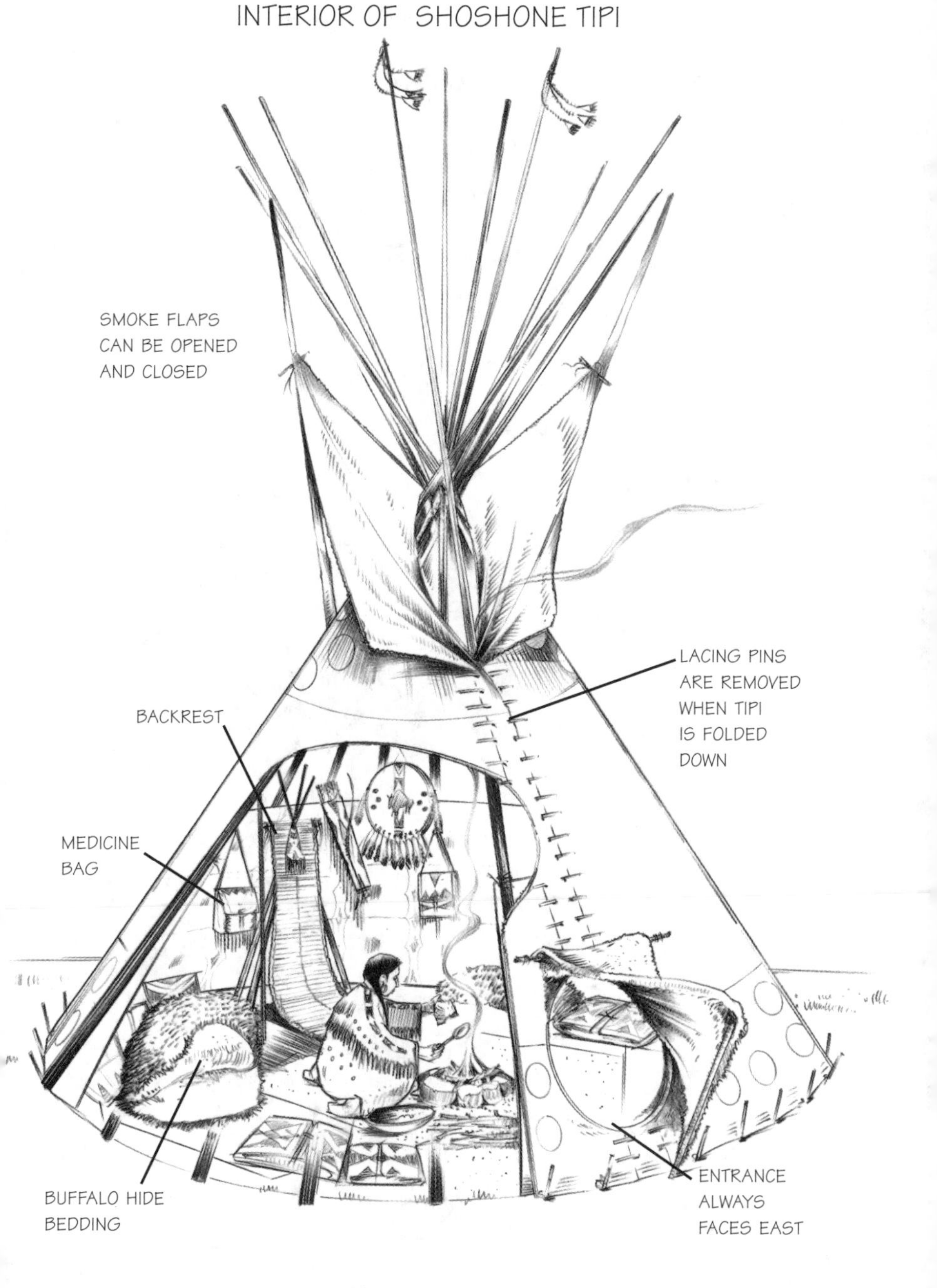

INTERIOR OF SHOSHONE TIPI

SMOKE FLAPS CAN BE OPENED AND CLOSED

LACING PINS ARE REMOVED WHEN TIPI IS FOLDED DOWN

BACKREST

MEDICINE BAG

BUFFALO HIDE BEDDING

ENTRANCE ALWAYS FACES EAST

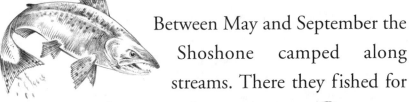

Between May and September the Shoshone camped along streams. There they fished for salmon and trout. In the fall, they packed their tipis onto horses. They then headed east to the plains of present-day Montana. There the men hunted buffalo, riding on horseback and using bows and arrows.

The weather was often very cold. So Shoshone men, women, and children needed lots of warm clothing. Sacagawea wore a dress and leggings that were made of deer skins. Over these went a knee-length robe made from buffalo hides. The robe became her blanket at night.

Her warm winter shoes were made from buffalo hide with the woolly hair on the inside. Her clothes were decorated with beads and porcupine quills.

BUFFALO HUNTIING

The American bison is also called the American buffalo. A large male bison is about the size of a small minivan. At the time of the Lewis and Clark Expedition, more than 50,000,000 bison roamed the Great Plains. The Shoshone and the other Plains Indians depended on them for food, warm clothing, and shelter. Their tipis were made from buffalo hides.

Whites began to settle on the Great Plains shortly after the expedition. The United States government tried to force the Indian tribes to live on the reservations—smaller pieces of land.

In the late 1800s, white buffalo hunters killed all but 550 American bison. Having lost their food and shelter, the Indians moved to the reservations.

During the mid-1900s, some bison were returned to the prairies. Today 150,000 bison live on ranches and in national parks in the United States and Canada.

The Shoshone did not have schools. Sacagawea learned by working beside the women of her tribe. She collected wood for fires. She helped make moccasins, clothing, and tipis. She picked berries and dug roots for her family to eat. She learned to make medicines from plants.

The village elders taught Sacagawea the beliefs of her people. She heard how the Creator made the world and Coyote made human beings.

She was warned about the Little People, who shot invisible arrows. For fun, she ran races and juggled mud balls with her friends.

Like all Shoshone girls, Sacagawea was promised to an older man. She would become his wife when she turned 13 or 14. But in 1800, her life changed forever.

Sacagawea was just 10 or 11 at the time. Her tribe was camped near what is now Three Forks, Montana.

Suddenly,
Minnetaree
Indians attacked.
This enemy tribe had
guns. The Shoshone had
only bows and arrows.
Fifteen of Sacagawea's people died in the attack.
The rest fled to the woods. The Minnetaree
chased them, taking women and children prisoner.
Sacagawea was running across a river

when a warrior grabbed her. He pulled her onto his horse and rode away. Her best friend was also captured.

Sacagawea and the other prisoners were taken 600 miles to a Minnetaree village in what is now North Dakota. Her friend escaped, but Sacagawea didn't. The young Shoshone girl was given to a Minnetaree family.

Sacagawea was a prisoner among strangers. She was hundreds of miles from home. She missed her family. She did not even know if they were still alive.

A fur trader from Canada often visited the village where Sacagawea now lived. His name was Toussaint Charbonneau (TOO sant Shar buh NO).

BUFFALO HEADDRESS
WITH EAGLE FEATHERS

Charbonneau was three times as old as Bird Woman. But when he saw her, he wanted her for his wife. The Minnetaree traded her to him. Just like that, Sacagawea became one of his Indian wives. Now she belonged to another stranger.

Sacagawea and her husband settled in a village of Mandan and Minnetaree Indians. By the age of about 15, she was expecting a child. Her baby was not yet born when some strangers arrived in the village. Once again, Bird Woman's life was about to change forever.

MANDAN EARTH LODGE

BUFFALO ROBE

THOMAS JEFFERSON

Thomas Jefferson (1743–1826) was born in Virginia's Albemarle County. His family owned a plantation and about twenty slaves.

In 1776, Jefferson wrote the Declaration of Independence. Soon after the United States became a nation, he tried to send out two expeditions to explore the American West. Both attempts failed. Jefferson became our nation's third president in 1801. In 1803, Congress granted President Jefferson $2,500 to explore North America. He sent out the Lewis and Clark Expedition from St. Louis late that summer.

President Jefferson served two terms as President, from 1801–1809. He later founded and built the University of Virginia. His personal library of 6,400 volumes became the core collection of the Library of Congress. Thomas Jefferson died on the Fourth of July, 1826.

Chapter 2
Visitors

Two centuries ago, the United States was much smaller than it is today. It only included the land from the Atlantic Ocean to the Mississippi River. The country got much bigger in 1803. That year, France sold our young nation 828,000 square miles of land west of the Mississippi. This was called the Louisiana Purchase. It doubled the country's size. The region was later divided into fifteen states.

Much of the new land was unexplored. What did it look like? Who lived there? What plants and animals might be found?

President Thomas Jefferson planned an expedition to head northwest to the Pacific Ocean. The

explorers would travel mainly by river. They would make maps of the land. They would trade with Indians along the way.

The voyagers would do more than visit the territory of the Louisiana Purchase. They would also explore what is now Idaho, Washington, and Oregon. Great Britain also had its eye on this territory. Jefferson wanted American explorers to get there first. That would strengthen U.S.

MERIWETHER LEWIS

claims to the region. Nobody stopped to think that the land already belonged to the Indians.

Two army men would lead the expedition. One was 29-year-old Meriwether Lewis. He was President Jefferson's friend and personal secretary. Lewis picked William Clark as his co-captain. The 33-year-old Clark was a tall, friendly man with red hair.

WILLIAM CLARK

Clark's first task was to find men for the expedition. He and Lewis needed men who could hunt and build boats and forts. They needed men who could handle horses. President Jefferson wanted a record of the trip. So men who could keep journals were also needed.

Most of what we know about Sacagawea has come from these journals.

Captain Clark gathered 43 men. They called themselves the Corps of Discovery. Several spoke French. One knew Indian sign language. Another played the violin. He could entertain the men when they were far from home. Clark's slave York also made the trip.

One member of the group had four feet: Captain Lewis brought along Seaman, his 140-pound Newfoundland dog.

On May 14, 1804, the Corps of Discovery set out from St. Louis. They began rowing up the Missouri River in a barge and two smaller boats. By late October—the time the Indians called the "Moon of the Falling Leaves"—the explorers had reached central North Dakota. This was where Sacagawea now lived with Charbonneau. The voyagers stopped in the area to camp for the winter. There they built a cluster of cabins, which they called "Fort Mandan."

Soon Charbonneau heard interesting news.

KEELBOAT

PIROGUE

Lewis and Clark were looking for one more person for their expedition. At one stage of their journey, they would need horses to help them cross the Bitterroot Mountains. They hoped to

TROPHY AND MEDICINE
POLES WERE LIKE FLAGS

get them from the Shoshone Indians, who were famous for their horse breeding. The explorers would need someone who could speak to the Shoshone.

Charbonneau brought his pregnant wife, Sacagawea, to meet Lewis and Clark. She could speak Shoshone, he told them. She was Shoshone. Charbonneau wanted to go along, too. He knew French and some Minnetaree. He could also help the explorers.

The captains asked Bird Woman and Charbonneau to join them. They agreed to pay the trader $500. In the early 1800s, this was a fortune. Sacagawea and her husband were now part of the Corps of Discovery. The couple moved into Fort Mandan for the winter. They shared a cabin with Lewis, Clark, and York.

On February 11, 1805, Bird Woman was about to have her baby. To hurry along the birth, she was given a special powder. It was made from a rattlesnake's tail. She drank it with water. Ten minutes later, she gave birth to a healthy baby boy.

INTERIOR OF MANDAN EARTH LODGE

PEOPLE OFTEN SAT ON
ROOF AND CHILDREN
PLAYED THERE

STORAGE AREA

SLEEPING AREA

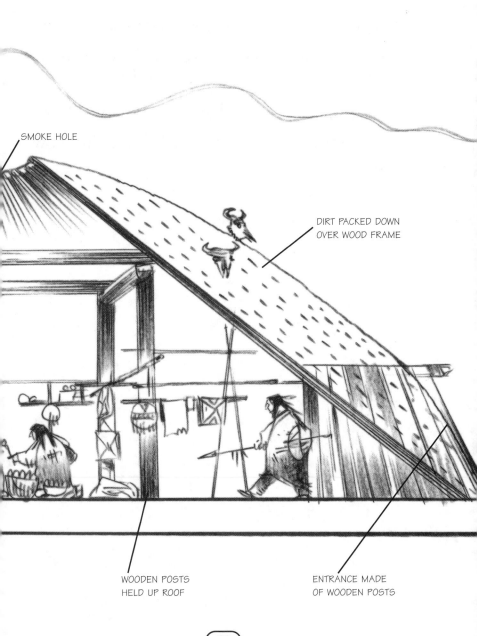

SMOKE HOLE

DIRT PACKED DOWN
OVER WOOD FRAME

WOODEN POSTS
HELD UP ROOF

ENTRANCE MADE
OF WOODEN POSTS

Charbonneau named the child Jean Baptiste (Jhan ba TEEST). Clark called the baby "Pomp." He called Sacagawea "Janey."

The captains hoped that Sacagawea would be of help on the long trip. They had no idea just how valuable she would be.

Chapter 3
Bird Woman's River

The winter of 1804–05 was very cold. At sunrise on January 9, it was 21 degrees below zero. The next morning, it was 40 below. No wonder the Indians called this time of year "Frost in the Tipi"! The people at Fort Mandan tried to stay warm and find food. But the hunters had little luck. Fortunately, Mandan Indians from nearby villages traded corn to the explorers.

CORN WAS EATEN RAW
OR DRIED AND STORED
FOR WINTER

The Mandan also showed the voyagers how they made blue glass beads. Indians called these "chief's beads." Tribes in the Northwest used them as money. The beads were also worn as hair decorations, earrings, and necklaces. Sacagawea had a belt of blue beads. It was her prized possession.

PRAIRIE DOGS WERE
A NEW DISCOVERY
TO LEWIS

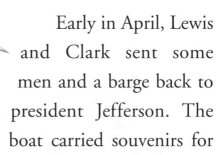

Early in April, Lewis and Clark sent some men and a barge back to president Jefferson. The boat carried souvenirs for the president. These included a prairie dog, four magpies, many newly discovered plants, and an Indian robe.

In the meantime, the men at Fort Mandan were busy. They built new boats so they could continue their long journey to the ocean. The boats were loaded with food and other supplies.

On April 7, the voyagers—including Sacagawea, Charbonneau, and Pomp—left Fort Mandan. They rowed up the Missouri River in six small

FROM THEIR WINTER HOME IN THE MANDAN
VILLAGE, THE EXPLORERS HEADED NORTHWEST
INTO UNCHARTED TERRITORY.

canoes and two pirogues. The pirogues were long,
narrow rowboats with sails.

As they paddled west, every traveler but one
was leaving home farther behind. Only Bird
Woman was heading toward home. For five years,
she had not seen her family or friends. She had
been enslaved—first by the Minnetaree, then

by Charbonneau. Now, thanks to Lewis and Clark, she was heading back to the land of her birth. Would she meet her people there? Were her family and friends still alive? What would they think of her baby?

Sometimes Sacagawea rode in one of the boats. Often, she walked along the shore with Clark. Pomp traveled in a cradle board on his mother's

back. At night, Bird Woman and her family shared a tent with the two captains and York. Clark came from a large, loving family. He quickly grew fond of Sacagawea and Pomp. And he soon saw that letting Sacagawea come along had been a very wise decision.

On their third day out of Fort Mandan, Sacagawea found some tasty wild artichokes while

on shore. She cooked these roots for dinner. Bird Woman found many kinds of plant foods during the expedition. Among them were currants and gooseberries.

Five weeks later, Sacagawea prevented a disaster. May 14, 1805, was very foggy. Lewis and Clark

were walking along the Missouri River. Bird Woman, with Pomp on her back, was in one of the pirogues. Her husband was steering. Several other men were also in the boat. They were 300 feet from shore.

Suddenly, a gust of wind upset the boat. It quickly filled with water. Charbonneau cried out that he couldn't swim. As the other men desperately bailed out the boat, Sacagawea saw their supplies floating away.

Clark later wrote in his journal:

A squall of wind struck our sail broadside and turned the pirogue nearly over....The articles which floated out were nearly all caught by [Sacagawea].... In this pirogue were our papers, instruments, books, medicine and, in short, almost every article necessary to insure the success of the enterprise.

Had she not saved the supplies, the expedition might have had to turn back.

The captains wanted to honor Sacagawea. So they named a creek in central Montana for her. "This stream we called...bird woman's River, after our interpreter the Snake Woman," wrote Lewis. On maps it is called the Sacagawea River.

The Missouri River became swifter and clearer as they approached the mountains. Cottonwood and willow trees lined the riverbanks. In the distance, pines and junipers topped the higher land. But higher land also meant colder temperatures. At night, water in the kettles crusted with ice—even though it was late May.

Rain and snow made traveling difficult. But there were plenty of deer and buffalo to hunt. The explorers stored the meat in their canoes.

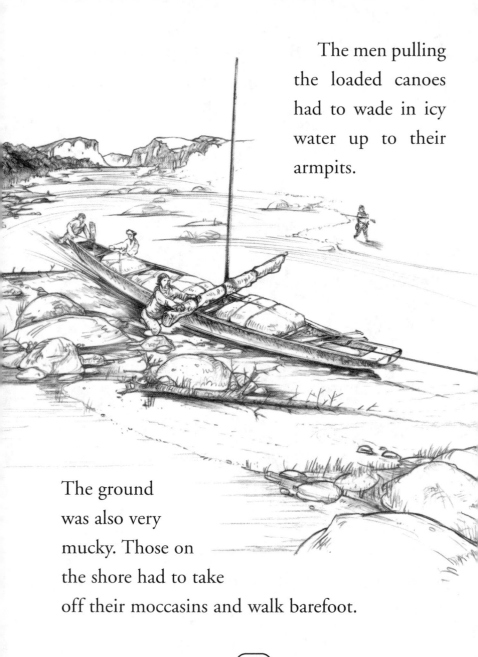

The men pulling the loaded canoes had to wade in icy water up to their armpits.

The ground was also very mucky. Those on the shore had to take off their moccasins and walk barefoot.

Hardly a day passed without problems. Captain Clark and Bird Woman were almost bitten by rattlesnakes. Mosquitoes stung the men and turned Pomp's little body into a mass of red sores. One man after another came down with flu, fevers, and diarrhea.

IN THE JEFFERSON RIVER, AS THE WATER BECAME SHALLOW, THE CORPS HAD TO PULL THEIR BOATS WITH CORDS MADE OF ELK HIDE.

Sacagawea began running a fever around June 1. As she grew worse, the captains feared that she would die. They were also afraid that the expedition would fail without her. How would they trade for horses without their Shoshone translator? Without horses, how would they get across the Bitterroot Mountains? And who would take care of Pomp if his mother died?

Clark wrote in his journal on June 16, 1805:

"The Indian woman verry bad,
&...out of her senses."

The captains took turns caring for Sacagawea. They gave her tea made of tree bark. They brought her iron-rich water from springs. Not until June 24 did she feel better.

By then, the expedition had reached the Great
Falls of the Missouri River. These waterfalls drop
400 feet. The voyagers could not go up the falls in
their boats. They had to drag their boats around
them. This is called "portaging."

They placed the boats on wheels made from slices of a tree trunk. The men then pushed and pulled the boats across the hard ground. Cactus thorns sliced the bottoms of their feet right through their moccasins. Grizzly bears sniffed around their camp at night. Lewis's dog, Seaman, barked all night to scare the bears away.

Then storms hit. The worst storm struck on June 29. Bird Woman, carrying Pomp, was walking along a dry creek bed. Charbonneau and Clark were with her.

As rain began to fall, the group hid under a rock shelf. The shower turned into a downpour. Suddenly, a flash flood roared down the ravine. In seconds, the rushing water was waist high.

Pushing Sacagawea and Pomp ahead of him, Clark scrambled up the steep bluff. Charbonneau pulled Sacagawea up by her hand. They escaped just before the ravine filled with 15 feet of water. Pomp's cradle board was swept away, but Sacagawea hung on to her baby.

Meanwhile, giant hailstones pounded the main camp. Several men were hurt. One man was knocked to the ground three times. Captain Lewis reported that the hailstones were as wide as seven inches. They bounced ten feet high after striking the ground.

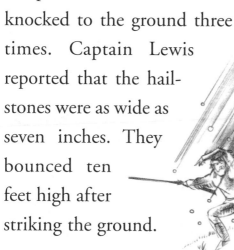

On July 1, the portage was completed. The falls were now behind them. The men made two new canoes Indian-style, burning and scraping out the insides of cottonwood trees. The voyagers continued up the Missouri River in their eight canoes.

By late July, the land began to look familiar to Sacagawea. Her excitement grew. After five years, she was coming back to her homeland! On July 22, they reached a creek. Sacagawea remembered that her people had camped in this very place. Soon after, she showed the men the exact spot where she had been kidnapped.

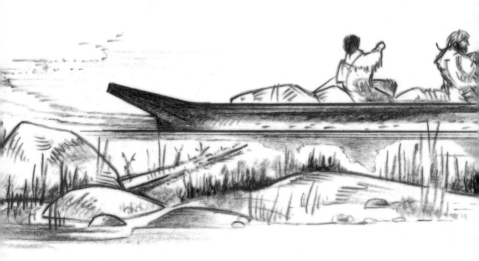

Days passed. There was still no sign of her people. The two captains grew desperate. They had counted on getting horses and guides from the Shoshone. If not, how would they cross the mountains? To make things worse, the men were exhausted. Their food was running low.

Sacagawea, however, remained hopeful. When they reached a rock known as the Beaver's Head, she was sure that the Shoshone must be nearby.

On August 1, the explorers split into two groups to look for Sacagawea's tribe. Lewis led a small group by land. Bird Woman and her family stayed with Clark and the rest of the men. They continued on by canoe.

Chapter 4
Coming Home

On the morning of August 13, 1805, Lewis and his three men spotted two Shoshone women and a girl. The Indians bowed their heads. They expected to be killed. But Lewis spoke to them kindly. He gave them beads and mirrors. As a sign of peace, he also painted the Indians' cheeks red. The three Shoshone agreed to take Captain Lewis and his men to their village.

They were on their way when 60 Shoshone warriors appeared on horses. They thundered toward Lewis and his men. Their chief got off his horse and greeted Lewis with a hug. He then took the four strangers to his village. There, the explorers and Indians smoked the peace pipe together.

Lewis asked the chief to come meet the rest of the explorers. A Shoshone woman was with them, Lewis said. The chief agreed to go. But his warriors feared that Lewis was leading them into a trap.

Meanwhile, Clark approached with the main group. Sacagawea was walking along a riverbank. Suddenly she saw several Indians on horses in the distance. Bird Woman stared at them. Then she began dancing with joy and sucking on her fingers. This was an Indian sign meaning "These are my people!"

The Shoshone warriors were happy to see Sacagawea, too. Now they knew that the white men meant no harm. Together, the Indians and the explorers headed toward the Shoshone village. When they were nearly there, a young woman pushed her way through the crowd. She hugged

Sacagawea. They began talking excitedly. Bird Woman had found her dearest friend. She was the girl who had escaped from the Minnetaree. Sacagawea had not seen her for five years.

At the village, the captains met with the chief. Sacagawea had to translate. She had barely sat down when she looked at the chief. Weeping with joy, she rushed to him and threw her blanket over him as a token of love. The Shoshone chief was her brother. It was Cameahwait!

Cameahwait was happy to be with his

long lost sister. The brother and sister talked a while. Then Bird Woman sat down to translate. She was so overjoyed at seeing her brother that she kept bursting into tears. But the chief had to act dignified.

Sacagawea explained that the captains needed horses. Asking even simple questions was very hard. That was because

they went from English to French to Minnetaree to Shoshone. The chief's answers went from Shoshone to Minnetaree to French and back to English. A deal was made. The explorers would give the Indians battle-axes, knives, and clothing. In exchange, the chief would supply horses and guides. Now the expedition had a way to cross the Bitterroot Mountains.

Sacagawea and the explorers spent several days with the Shoshone. Sacagawea learned some very sad news. Most of her family was dead. Cameahwait, another brother, and her sister's little boy were her only living relatives. Bird Woman must have been tempted to stay with her people. However, she chose to move on with the Corps of Discovery. We can only guess why. Perhaps she felt loyal to the explorers. They had treated her and Pomp kindly. She may have never felt so important before. The chance to visit other Indian tribes and see the ocean must have also been exciting to a young girl.

The explorers were still among the Shoshone when Bird Woman overheard something shocking. Her brother had changed his mind. He was going to break his promise. He was going to keep the horses and take his hungry people to hunt buffalo. Sacagawea told Charbonneau what she had learned. She asked him to tell Captain Lewis.

Lewis confronted
Cameahwait. The chief was ashamed. He would
keep his word after all, he said. Once again,
Sacagawea had helped save the expedition.
Without horses, the explorers could not have
continued westward.

A *TRAVOIS* WAS USED
TO CARRY LOADS.
DOGS OR HORSES
PULLED THEM.

In late August—the Moon When the
Geese Shed Their Feathers—Sacagawea
said farewell to her family and
friends. Now it was time for the
explorers to start climbing the Bitterroots.

Chapter 5
To the Pacific

Crossing the Bitterroots was difficult and dangerous. It began snowing. The ground was so slippery that several horses fell. Food was so scarce that Clark named a river Hungry Creek.

Sacagawea was still nursing her baby and needed food badly. So did the men. Some were so ill they could barely walk. The hungry travelers had to kill and eat a few of their horses.

The mountain crossing lasted until late September. On the prairie below, the explorers met many Nez Perce Indians. They traded with them for food. They stuffed themselves with berries, dried salmon, and bread made from camas roots. Captain Clark was one of those who ate too much. "I am very sick today and puke which relieves me," he wrote.

Now that they had crossed the mountains, the explorers did not need their horses until their return trip.

The Nez Perce agreed to take care of the animals until then. Near what is now Orofino, Idaho, the travelers made five new canoes. In early October, they resumed their journey.

They paddled on toward the Pacific
Ocean. Once again, they ran out of food.
They bought two dozen dogs from Indians
and ate them.

In what is now eastern Washington,
they reached the Columbia River. All
along this great river they met Indians.
An all-male group would have alarmed the
tribes. But when the Indians saw Bird Woman and

Pomp, they welcomed the travelers. "No woman ever accompanies a war party," Clark explained in his journal.

As they neared the Pacific, rain began to fall. It rained day after day. The Columbia River grew so wild that the voyagers felt seasick. Huge logs, dashing against the shore, nearly crushed their canoes. The rain filled their boat and rotted their clothing.

Also there were fleas. The fleas got inside what

was left of the voyagers'
clothes. The men were so itchy
that they took off their rags
and rowed naked!

Then came the moment
they had long awaited. They
could smell the ocean. On November 7, 1805,
they saw the ocean! Sacagawea and her baby had
come more than 2,200 miles for this sight.

CEDAR LODGE

CHIEF WEARING
CARVED WOOD
HELMET AND
GOAT WOOL ROBE

For nearly a month, the explorers camped along the Columbia River's north shore. They were looking for a good place to spend the winter. But the rain did not let up.

The men had trouble finding wood dry enough to start a fire. Bird Woman could not keep herself and Pomp warm or dry.

One evening in late November, a Chinook Indian chief visited the camp. He wore a cape made of sea-otter skins. Lewis wanted that cape. The explorers had spent all of their blue beads. Lewis offered the chief two blankets for the cape.

"I would not trade my coat for five such blankets," he answered.

Then the chief saw Sacagawea's beautiful belt of blue beads. He wanted it as much as Captain Lewis wanted the cape. Bird Woman was forced to hand over her belt. Lewis got his cape. The captains gave Sacagawea a blue cloth coat in exchange, but her treasure was gone.

By late November, the explorers had to pick a site for their winter quarters. They took a vote. Everyone, including Bird Woman and Clark's slave York, voted on where to build their fort. This was one of the rare times in this period of history that a woman or a slave was allowed to have an equal vote with white men.

Sacagawea wanted to move to the other side of the Columbia River. A tasty root was available there. "Janey in favour of a place where there is plenty of [wapato]," Clark wrote. Most of the men also wanted to move across the river, where they could hunt elk. The expedition crossed the Columbia. As they did, they passed from Washington to Oregon.

Near present-day Astoria, Oregon, the explorers
began to build their winter home. They called it

"Fort Clatsop" because the Clatsop Indians lived nearby.

Most of December 1805 was spent building Fort Clatsop. They had picked a good spot. There was enough wood to build the fort. It had six rooms, each with a fireplace. The land was high enough to keep from flooding in the constant rain. Elk were plentiful. These animals provided meat as well as skins for new clothes.

Chapter 6
Winter 1805–06

While at Fort Clatsop, the explorers made more than 300 pairs of moccasins for the trip home. A pair of moccasins lasted just a few days.

The explorers traded with the Clatsop tribe for cakes made of berries and for other foods. The nearby ocean also had something valuable—salt. It was needed to flavor food and preserve meat for the return trip.

SALT POURED
INTO WOODEN
BARRELS

STONE OVEN

To make salt, the men boiled seawater in large
kettles. When the water bubbled away, salt stuck
to the sides of the pots. Then the men scraped off
the salt and stored it.

CARRYING BUCKETS
OF SEA WATER

Around New Year's Day of 1806, the captains heard that a whale had washed up on the coast. Clark formed a group to get its oil and blubber. The blubber tasted like pork fat. This would be a treat for people who had eaten only wapato and elk for weeks.

No one thought of including Bird Woman on the trip to see the whale. She felt hurt. She had traveled a great distance under terrible conditions with the men. She had saved their supplies. She had helped get them horses, found food for them, and risked her life several times. And she had done

all this while caring for her baby. She wanted to see the whale.

Through her translation chain, Sacagawea spoke to Clark. "I have traveled a long way to see the great waters," she told him. "Now that you are going to see the monstrous fish, I think it very hard that I cannot go." Captain Clark took Bird Woman along to see the whale.

Pomp's birthday fell on February 11, 1806. By then, he was starting to say a few words and to walk. Clark had grown to love the child. He called him "my little dancing boy." Before Pomp went to sleep at night, Clark held him and sang to him.

Early spring brought more excitement to Fort Clatsop. The Corps had spent three and a half months in their winter quarters. Now it was time to head back home.

On March 22, 1806, Lewis and Clark gave their fort to the Clatsop Indian chief.

The next afternoon, they began their journey back to St. Louis.

BRITISH TERR

COLUMBIA

REUNION
POINT

MANDAN
VILLAGE

OREGON
COUNTRY

FORT CLATSOP
(1806)

SNAKE

MISSOURI RIVER

LEWIS TAKES NORTHERN
ROUTE — CLARK TAKES
SOUTHERN ROUTE

LOUISIANA
PURCHASE
1803

S
L

N

W   E

S

RETURN TRIP
TO SAINT LOUIS
1805-1806

Chapter 7
The Return Trip

The return trip wasn't quite as hard as the journey to the sea had been. Still, the travelers were often hungry and ill.

Sacagawea's skill at finding plant foods was needed more than ever. She gathered wild onions and roots for the voyagers. One such root was camas. This plant has flowers so blue that a field of camas looks like a lake.

CAMAS

She also found plants that she used as medicine. "Our sick men are much better today," Lewis wrote on May 16, 1806. "Sahcargarweah gathered a quantity of the roots of a species of fennel, which we found very agreeable...."

During the Moon When the Ponies Shed—also known as May—the explorers returned to the Nez Perce Indians. They took back the horses they had left there. They needed them for the journey back over the mountains.

Also in May, Pomp got sick. The 15-month-old child ran a high fever. His neck and throat were swollen. Bird Woman and the captains rubbed his

POMPEYS PILLAR

neck with boiled onions and beeswax. Soon Pomp was all better.

For part of the trip the two captains split up. Sacagawea traveled with Clark. She did not meet her tribe on the way home. Yet Bird Woman knew the land that they passed through. She showed Clark the best way through the mountains. "The indian woman…has been of great service to me as a pilot through this country," he wrote.

On July 25, 1806, Clark's group saw a huge rock near what is now Billings, Montana. It was

200 feet high—as tall as a 20-story building.
Captain Clark named it Pompey's Tower for the
child who had been so ill. Clark climbed the rock
and carved his name and the date on it. Today
the rock is called "Pompeys Pillar." Clark also
named a nearby stream for his "little dancing boy."
This stream is known as "Pompeys Pillar Creek."

Lewis's group joined up with Clark's on
August 12. They met near the Montana—North

Dakota border. The travelers then floated back down the Missouri River in their canoes. Soon they reached the village where the explorers had met Sacagawea two winters earlier.

The captains paid Charbonneau $500.33. This equaled two years' pay for a worker at that time.

Now the time had come for Sacagawea, Charbonneau, and little Pomp to say good-bye to all the explorers.

The Corps of Discovery then glided downriver from their starting point, St. Louis. They had covered eight thousand miles and had been away for twenty-eight months. They hadn't been heard from for so long that most Americans assumed they were dead.

As they neared St. Louis, the men began to celebrate. Their long journey was almost over. Soon they would see their families again.

The Lewis and Clark expedition reached St. Louis in late September. Cheering crowds greeted the men. They were heroes. They had explored

vast and distant lands. Lewis and Clark had paved the way for America's settlement of the west.

WILLIAM CLARK

William Clark (1770–1838) was born in Caroline County, Virginia. His family, like Jefferson's and Lewis', was from Albemarle County. In 1783, his older brother, George Rogers Clark, became Thomas Jefferson's first choice to lead a cross-country exploration. George declined. Twenty years later, William co-captained the Lewis and Clark Expedition.

Captain William Clark had spent four years in the army. He was a skilled boatman, mapmaker, and frontiersman. His lively journals from the Lewis and Clark Expedition tell the day-to-day events of the trip.

After the famous journey, Clark made his home in St. Louis. He became the nation's Superintendent of Indian Affairs. He married and named his first son Meriwether Lewis Clark. William Clark also raised and educated Sacagawea's children, Jean Baptiste (Pomp) and Lisette.

MERIWETHER LEWIS

Meriwether Lewis (1774–1809) was born on a Virginia plantation near Thomas Jefferson's farm, Monticello. His father and Jefferson were good friends as well as neighbors.

In 1794, Lewis volunteered as a soldier. The next year he joined a sharpshooter company led by Captain William Clark.

When Thomas Jefferson became President in 1801, Lewis moved into the White House as his personal aide. Two years later, President Jefferson appointed him to lead the expedition to explore the American West. Lewis asked his former commander, Captain Clark, to be his co-captain.

After the expedition, Lewis was named governor of the Louisiana Territory. Lewis did a poor job. He was a heavy drinker. The woman he loved married someone else. He owed money to several friends.

On October 11, 1809, Meriwether Lewis shot himself to death.

Chapter 8
What Became of Bird Woman?

And what became of the young Shoshone woman? Sacagawea had made one of the most remarkable journeys in American history. She had traveled 4,500 miles carrying her baby on her back. Without her, the expedition might have failed. Yet she wasn't paid one penny.

For a while, Bird Woman, Pomp, and Charbonneau stayed at the Indian village. There,

Charbonneau received a letter from Clark. Clark missed them. He missed Pomp most of all. Clark planned

SACAGAWEA CARRIED HER BABY IN A CRADLEBOARD. IT HAD A STIFF RAWHIDE BACK AND A SOFT LACED POUCH TO HOLD THE BABY.

to settle in St. Louis. He wanted Charbonneau to move his family there, too. Did Charbonneau want land for a farm near St. Louis? Did he want to start a small business? Clark would help him. But what Clark really wanted was to adopt Pomp. The captain wrote a letter to the couple:

As to your little son (my boy Pomp) you well know my fondness for him.... I once more tell you that if you will bring your son...to me, I will educate him and treat him as my own child....

Sacagawea, her husband, and Pomp eventually did go to St. Louis. In the autumn of 1810, Charbonneau bought a small farm from Clark. For five months, Bird Woman and Pomp lived there. But Charbonneau soon grew restless. The next spring, he took Sacagawea on a fur-trading trip up the Missouri River. Six-year-old Pomp was left in St. Louis. He was cared for by William Clark and his wife, Julia.

By late 1812, Bird Woman and Charbonneau were at a trading post in what is now South Dakota. Sacagawea died there on December 20, 1812. She had just given birth to a daughter named Lisette.

The clerk at the fort recorded the sad news:

This evening the wife of Charbonneau, a Snake [woman], died of a putrid fever. She was a good and the best woman in the fort, aged about 25 years. She left a fine infant girl.

Clark took the baby girl, Lisette, too. He raised both of Sacagawea's children. Pomp became a well-known Western guide and trader. Later he was the mayor of a Spanish town in California. What became of Lisette is not known.

Chapter 9
Honoring Sacagawea

For nearly a century after the Lewis and Clark expedition, Sacagawea was largely forgotten. During the 1800s, Indians and whites fought many wars. White people did not want to honor any Native American.

By 1900, the fighting had ended. The country was getting ready to celebrate the expedition's 100th anniversary. That was when Americans "discovered" Bird Woman. Suddenly, she became very well-known. Sacagawea has had more landmarks named for her and memorials built in her honor than any other American woman.

Idaho, Montana, Oregon, and Wyoming have mountains named for Sacagawea. Washington and North Dakota have lakes named for her.

STATUE IN STATE
HOUSE GARDEN,
BISMARCK
NORTH DAKOTA

SACAGAWEA

She also became a favorite subject of artists and writers. Nobody knows what she looked like, so artists have had to use their imaginations. A statue of her stands at the State Capitol in

Bismarck, North Dakota. A statue of Sacagawea and Pomp will soon be placed in the U.S. Capitol Building in Washington, D.C.

As the 21st century approached, the U.S. Mint planned to issue a new dollar coin. Sacagawea would appear on its "heads" side. Twenty-three artists sent in designs for the golden dollar. The Mint showed the final choices on its Web site. More than 120,000 Americans voted for their favorites by E-mail. Many of them were school-children.

The golden Sacagawea dollars came out in 2000. It shows a young Indian woman carrying her baby. This coin begins a period of Lewis and Clark celebrations. The years 2004-2006 will mark the expedition's 200th anniversary. Americans will honor the explorers for their historic journey to the sea. And they will remember the young Shoshone woman who helped them get there. Sacagawea.

Timeline of Sacagawea's Life

1789	Possible year Sacagawea was born. The exact date is not known.
1790	Possible year Sacagawea was born. The exact date is not known.
1800	Minataree Indians attack the Shoshone tribe's camp. Sacagawea is captured and traded to a man from Canada (Toussaint Charbonneau). She becomes his wife.
1803	"Louisiana Purchase" doubles the country's size.
1804	Lewis and Clark and the Corps of Discovery set out from St. Louis to explore the new land.
1805	Sacagawea's son, Pomp, is born.
1806	Fort Clatsop is built.
1812	December 20. Possible date of Sacagawea's death.
2000	The United States issues a new dollar coin with Sacagawea pictured on it.

WORLD EVENTS

George Washington is elected as the first President of the United States. — **1789**

Jacob Schweppe begins the first carbonated beverage company in Switzerland — **1790**

The United States government moves from Philadelphia to its new capitol—Washington, D.C. — **1800**

Napoleon proclaims himself Emperor of France. Ludwig van Beethoven writes his Third Symphony. — **1804**

The first covered bridge is built in America. — **1805**

Webster's Dictionary is first published. — **1806**

Louisiana becomes the eighteenth state. Charles Dickens, author, is born. — **1812**

George W. Bush is declared the president-elect more than a month after Election Day. Hillary Rodham Clinton becomes the first First Lady to ever be elected to public office when she joins the U.S. Senate. — **2000**